A PERSPECTIVES FLIP BOOK

The Split History of the

CIVIL RIGHTS MOVEMENT

ACTIVISTS' PERSPECTIVE

BY NADIA HIGGINS

CONTENT CONSULTANT:
Zoe Burkholder, PhD
Assistant Professor, College of Education and Human Services
Montclair State University

COMPASS POINT BOOKS
a capstone imprint

Compass Point Books are published by Capstone,
1710 Roe Crest Drive, North Mankato, Minnesota 56003
www.capstonepub.com

LIBRARY OF CONGRESS CATALOGING-IN-PUBLICATION DATA

Cataloging information on file with the Library of Congress.
978-0-7565-4736-3 (library binding)
978-0-7565-4792-9 (paperback)
978-0-7565-4798-1 (eBook PDF)

EDITOR
BRENDA HAUGEN

LIBRARY CONSULTANT
KATHLEEN BAXTER

DESIGNER
ASHLEE SUKER

PRODUCTION SPECIALIST
LAURA MANTHE

MEDIA RESEARCHER
WANDA WINCH

Printed and bound in the USA.
072017   010671R

Table of Contents

FREEDOM IS POSSIBLE

Old ways were changing in the South, but it took the murder of a 14-year-old boy from Chicago, Illinois, to bring it to light. Emmett Till was visiting family in the small town of Money, Mississippi. One August evening in 1955 Emmett flirted with a white cashier on a dare. "Bye, baby," he said to Carolyn Bryant.

Three days later Bryant's husband, Roy, and his half-brother J.W. Milam showed up where Emmett was staying. Emmett's great-uncle, Moses Wright, saw the men grab Emmett and shove him in their truck. That night, August 28, they savagely beat the teen before shooting him and dumping his body in a river.

Emmett Till and his mother, Mamie Till Bradley

Lynchings of black men were common in Mississippi, and officials nearly always looked the other way. But Mamie Till Bradley would not let the murder of her son be ignored. She insisted on an open coffin at his funeral. After *Jet* magazine ran photos of his mangled face, Emmett Till became a rallying cry for outraged African-Americans.

An all-white jury found Bryant and Milam not guilty of murder. Their trial is still remembered, however, for the testimony of Moses Wright. "Thar he," said the old man, pointing at the attackers. For perhaps the first time ever, a black man in Mississippi had stood up to white men in a court of law.

THE "NEW NEGRO"

For years many black southerners didn't question why they were treated as second-class citizens. After all, whites had the best houses and schools. They ran government and businesses. Wasn't that proof of their superiority?

In truth, southern society oppressed blacks on several fronts — by law, custom, and by violence and intimidation. Jim Crow laws kept them from attending the best schools, going to libraries, or even trying on clothes at department stores. African-Americans used separate "colored" toilets, drinking fountains, bus stations, and more, instead of the same facilities white people did.

Few blacks were able to follow through on their constitutional right to vote. Special taxes and tests kept them from registering. If those tactics didn't work, the threat of a lynching did. Blacks who insisted on improving their lives were often punished by being fired from their jobs or getting evicted from their homes.

With World War II (1939–1945), however, blacks began to see their situation in a new light. African-American soldiers witnessed a larger world where races freely mixed. After defeating injustice abroad, the "new negro" returned ready to fight injustice at home.

THE MONTGOMERY BUS BOYCOTT

Many black workers in Montgomery, Alabama, relied on city buses to take them to their jobs. A black passenger entered the front of a bus to pay the fare. Then he or she would step off the bus and enter again from the back, where the "colored" seats were. Seats in the

Rosa Parks was arrested and fingerprinted after refusing to give up her seat on a bus.

front were reserved for whites. However, if the front was full, black riders in the back were to give up their seats for whites.

Rosa Parks was riding the bus home from work December 1, 1955, when she was ordered to forfeit her seat. Instead, 42-year-old Parks defiantly slid over to the window. With that, she was arrested.

Four days later Montgomery's buses rumbled through city streets mostly empty. The black community had organized a boycott. They would not set foot on city buses again until they could choose their own seats. Leading the effort was Martin Luther King Jr., a 26-year-old preacher.

That night King addressed a large meeting at the Holt Street Baptist Church. "For many years we have shown amazing patience," King told the cheering crowd. "But we come here tonight

Martin Luther King Jr. speaks about the Montgomery bus boycott.

to be saved from that patience that makes us patient with anything less than freedom and justice."

The boycott went on for 381 days. Some maids walked 7 or 8 miles (11 to 13 kilometers) to work each way, despite jeering from passersby. Boycotters squeezed into cars, even after their carpool meeting spots were dynamited. After King's own house was bombed, he insisted that protesters stay committed to nonviolent methods.

The U.S. Supreme Court delivered victory to the boycotters in November 1956. King and other leaders sat in the front of the first integrated bus in Montgomery on December 21, 1956. That ride symbolized one of the first grassroots victories of the civil rights movement.

INTO THE SCHOOLS

The U.S. Supreme Court had ruled in 1954 that segregated schools were unequal and therefore unconstitutional. The *Brown v. Board of Education* ruling was to provide black youth a fresh start. In reality, putting the law into practice would prove a long, hard struggle.

Nine black teenagers in Little Rock, Arkansas, found themselves in the national spotlight in 1957. The teenagers had enrolled at their city's best high school, the all-white Central High. Not long before Arkansas Governor Orval Faubus had helped usher in the first

Elizabeth Eckford is yelled at outside Central High School.

black students to the state's white colleges. So the Little Rock Nine, as the teenagers came to be known, looked on in disbelief as Faubus changed his political stripes. The teenagers became his chance to prove to voters that he was not "soft" on race.

With Faubus leading the way, a mob mentality grew among white supremacists in and around Little Rock. By early September the situation was so tense that the teenagers agreed to a plan to try to safely enter the school together. But Elizabeth Eckford's family did not own a phone, and she was accidently left out of the arrangement.

On the morning of September 4, Elizabeth prayed with her family to calm her nerves, and then she headed off to school. As Elizabeth stepped off a city bus, she saw an angry crowd surrounding her school. But she focused on the armed soldiers lining the streets, figuring they would help her through the crowd.

As Elizabeth neared the school doors, the National Guardsmen blocked her way. "Lynch her! Lynch her!" someone yelled, while another spat on her.

None of the black students attended school that day. They tried again September 23, only to be met by another violent mob. Finally, President Dwight D. Eisenhower sent federal help. The Little Rock Nine were taken to school under armed protection September 25. Paratroopers lined the street in front of the building, and helicopters roared overhead. The angry throng was kept at bay.

Eight of the nine teenagers made it through the school year, with Ernest Green graduating. Melba Pattillo Beals later said she was engulfed by a "stark, raving, compelling fear" that whole year. The black students were taunted, tripped, and pushed down stairs.

The next year Faubus closed Little Rock's public high schools rather than see them integrated. For a year every high school student had to find another way to go to school. When Central reopened only two of the Little Rock Nine returned. In the meantime, Faubus had been re-elected by a landslide. The civil rights movement seemed to be foundering.

STUDENTS LEAD THE WAY

*F*our black college students in Greensboro, North Carolina,

opened a new chapter in the civil rights movement February 1,

1960. They began with a simple but profound action — sitting

where they weren't allowed. That afternoon the young men arrived

downtown at the Woolworth's department store. They purchased

a few small items to show they were paying customers. Then, with

pounding hearts, the neatly dressed teenagers took four stools at the

store's whites-only lunch counter.

The waitress refused to serve them. Still, the Greensboro Four,

as they came to be called, stayed put. They remained seated for an

Young men wait to be served during the second day of the sit-in at the Woolworth lunch counter in Greensboro.

In the following days, hundreds of others followed the lead of the Greensboro Four. Soon the sit-ins, as the protests were called, spread like wildfire to cities across the South. Black students brushed past "Whites Only" signs at lunch counters, pools, libraries, and more. Unlike the Montgomery boycotters or the Little Rock Nine, these protesters were breaking the law.

At workshops in Nashville, Tennessee, students trained in this form of protest, called civil disobedience. Activists learned how to protect their heads during a beating or throw their bodies in front of a comrade who was being attacked. They were given a list of dos and don'ts: Do be courteous, sit straight, and face the counter. Don't laugh, strike back, or curse.

Sit-ins often turned dangerous. The students were beaten, spat on, or burned with cigarettes or hot coffee. Police dragged them off their stools and shoved them into paddy wagons. As one group got carted off, another group took its place.

"Jail, no bail," was the students' motto. They refused to pay a fee to escape imprisonment. Filling up jails was part of the strategy to cause as much inconvenience and expense to a city or county as possible. The activists also considered time in jail an honorable duty.

FREEDOM RIDES

As southern lunch counters became integrated, sit-ins began winding down. By 1961 the civil rights movement needed another jolt. James Farmer, director of the Congress of Racial Equality (CORE), had just the plan.

STUDENTS AND CIVIL RIGHTS

Having college students as leaders in the civil rights movement made sense. Since they had no jobs to lose and no families to support, they could afford to risk time in jail. Students had not been bullied by decades of segregation either.

At first students considered forming a youth arm of Martin Luther King's group, the Southern Christian Leadership Conference (SCLC). But they voted to form their own group in April 1960, the Student Nonviolent Coordinating Committee (SNCC). Called "Snick" after the group's initials, its tactics were more daring than King's organization. SNCC workers would risk their lives during the Freedom Rides in 1961. SNCC's focus was more grassroots as well. Its mission was to work with ordinary citizens instead of community leaders.

Bus station waiting rooms were segregated in the South.

The U.S. Supreme Court had banned segregation on buses and in waiting rooms that served interstate travelers. But in reality whites-only areas were still the common practice. CORE planned a Freedom Ride to bring the matter national attention. A group of riders, both black and white, would turn segregation on its head during a bus tour of the South. Whites would sit in the back of the bus, blacks in front. At terminals whites would use "colored" facilities, while blacks would head for whites-only ones.

Farmer understood the danger of such an idea. "We planned the Freedom Ride with the specific intention of creating a crisis," Farmer later recalled. But as the riders headed into the Deep South, they faced violence that shocked even him.

A group of Freedom Riders found a mob waiting for them in Birmingham, Alabama, on May 14, 1961. As they stepped off the bus, riders were beaten with bats, bottles, bicycle chains, and pipes. The mob attacked them for 15 minutes before police arrived.

It looked as if violence would put an end to the Freedom Rides. All but one of the battered CORE riders headed out of Alabama on an airplane. Only Nashville student leader John Lewis stepped up to continue the next leg of the ride. After writing their wills, 10 more students joined him.

The Freedom Riders went to Montgomery May 20 and were met by another mob. Alabama Governor John Patterson refused to protect the riders. Federal forces were sent to Montgomery to protect citizens acting on a freedom granted by the U.S. Supreme Court.

That summer the Freedom Rides continued without further mob attacks. By November 1 more than 300 whites-only signs were removed from bus stations. Among ordinary black southerners, Freedom Rider became the words to describe any civil rights worker.

Twenty years after his 1960s activism, John Lewis was elected to Congress.

ROADBLOCKS AND RENEWAL

*T*he sit-ins had focused on lunch counters; the Freedom Rides

targeted bus stations. Could segregation be swept from a whole

town? Student leader Charles Sherrod thought the experiment was

worth trying. The Student Nonviolent Coordinating Committee

began training activists in the small town of Albany, Georgia, in the

fall of 1961.

In the following months, Albany activists marched to the

bus terminal and to city hall. They applied for library cards and

boycotted city buses. They were dragged by the dozen to the county

jail. Martin Luther King Jr. joined the activists in jail after leading a

Police carry a demonstrator down the steps of the Albany Carnegie Library.

The Albany movement was using tried-and-true methods — but without success. City officials would not budge. Plus the activists had met a wily opponent in Albany's police chief, Laurie Pritchett. He instructed his officers to be gentle with the protesters. Instead of sending in federal assistance, President John F. Kennedy's administration praised Pritchett for his restraint.

Meanwhile, the press was reporting about fighting among the civil rights movement's three main groups: SNCC, King's Southern Christian Leadership Conference, and the National Association for the Advancement of Colored People (NAACP). King left

Albany defeated and depressed in August 1962. Still, the movement had learned some hard-earned lessons: Businesses made better targets than government, and only a crisis would push the federal government to act.

The SCLC chose Birmingham, Alabama, as the staging ground for its next offensive. This deeply segregated city was home to the infamous Eugene "Bull" Connor, Birmingham's powerful public safety commissioner. Dubbed "Project C" (for confrontation), the SCLC's plan relied on Connor's brutality to shake up the country and compel federal officials to intervene.

SCLC leaders spent weeks mapping out their strategy. Then, on April 2, King received a troubling phone call. Connor had been voted out of office, and a moderate segregationist was to take his place. King was pressured from all sides to back off and give the new official a chance, but King refused. In King's view the new official was just a more presentable version of Connor.

As it turned out, Connor stubbornly kept his job anyway. With the city government in turmoil, the SCLC moved forward. Activists picketed and boycotted the downtown stores. King led prayer marches to the steps of city hall. On Good Friday Bull Connor arrested King and carted him to jail, just as King had planned.

THE CHILDREN'S CRUSADE

As Birmingham's jails filled, the movement was running out of demonstrators. The Reverend James Bevel had an idea—recruit the city's black children. They didn't have any adult responsibilities

LETTER FROM A BIRMINGHAM JAIL

Martin Luther King Jr. was sharply criticized for moving forward with Project C instead of waiting to negotiate with Bull Connor's replacement. Local white clergymen took out a full-page ad in the *Birmingham News* accusing King of being a troublemaker. In jail King wrote a response to the ad.

King's "Letter from a Birmingham Jail" became one of most iconic documents of the civil rights movement. In the letter King eloquently explained his philosophy of nonviolence: "You may well ask: 'Why direct action? Why sit-ins, marches and so forth? Isn't negotiation a better path?' You are quite right in calling for negotiation. Indeed, this is the very purpose of direct action. Nonviolent direct action seeks to create such a crisis and foster such a tension that a community which has constantly refused to negotiate is forced to confront the issue. It seeks so to dramatize the issue that it can no longer be ignored."

Martin Luther King Jr. (seated) and the Reverend Ralph Abernathy were also jailed in Florida after a civil rights demonstration.

A 17-year-old activist is attacked by police dogs during a demonstration in Birmingham.

to hold them back. Plus the sight of children being dragged to jail would surely reach the nation's conscience.

Children ages 6 to 18 stayed out of school to demonstrate on May 2, 1963—and Connor took the bait. By the end of the day, school buses carted 959 singing children to city jails. The next morning more than 1,000 children gathered at Kelly Ingram Park, but they never got the chance to march. As news cameras clicked, snarling police dogs lunged at the children. Then Connor's men turned on the fire hoses. The powerful spray knocked the children over and slammed them into parked cars and against buildings.

The whole world was shocked by the images from Ingram Park. An alarmed President Kennedy stepped in to work out a deal between King and the city's business leaders. The two sides announced an agreement the following week.

By targeting businesses and creating a crisis, Project C had reversed the failure of Albany. That summer 50 cities in the South desegregated just to avoid becoming the next Birmingham.

"I HAVE A DREAM"

African-Americans rejoiced as President Kennedy told the nation in June 1963 of his plans to create a federal law to end segregation. Still, the controversial bill could be defeated in Congress. The movement would have to mobilize behind the law.

About 250,000 people flocked to Washington, D.C., for the March on Washington for Jobs and Freedom August 28, 1963. Standing in front of the Lincoln Memorial, Martin Luther King Jr gave the most famous speech of his career. "I have a dream," King's voice rang out, "that my four little children will one day live in a nation where they will not be judged by the color of their skin, but by the content of their character. I have a dream today!" On that summer day, amid a sea of hopeful faces—black and white—King's dream felt closer than ever.

Martin Luther King delivers his "I Have a Dream" speech.

THE FIGHT FOR VOTING RIGHTS

CH. 5

*P*resident Lyndon Johnson was on the cusp of signing

the Civil Rights Act in June 1964. The law would ban racial

discrimination in public life, but the right to vote remained elusive.

The Constitution protected African-Americans' right to vote

in theory. But in reality black voters were thwarted in some

communities by local laws and customs. African-Americans lined

up at voter registration offices only to be turned away by "Closed"

signs. If they did get through the lines, they were subjected to unfair

tests. "How many bubbles are there in a cake of soap?" they might

be asked, only to be deemed unfit to vote.

President Lyndon Johnson signs the 1964 Civil Rights Act.

But few African-Americans even dared trying to register to vote. A simple walk to city hall could make a black person a target for lynching. Nowhere was this truer than in Mississippi.

SNCC leader Bob Moses knew the ability to vote was key. Black voters electing black leaders was the only way to ensure a power shift in Mississippi. He organized a massive voter registration project in 1964 called Freedom Summer. Hundreds of northern volunteers—most of them white college students—would knock on doors across the state. They would also canvass for a new political party, the Mississippi Freedom Democratic Party (MFDP). The party would challenge the state's whites-only Democratic Party at the national convention in August.

In mid-June the volunteers underwent training in Oxford, Ohio, where they learned basic survival strategies. They were told not to

THE FBI IS SEEKING INFORMATION CONCERNING THE DISAPPEARANCE AT PHILADELPHIA, MISSISSIPPI, OF THESE THREE INDIVIDUALS ON JUNE 21, 1964. EXTENSIVE INVESTIGATION IS BEING CONDUCTED TO LOCATE GOODMAN, CHANEY, AND SCHWERNER, WHO ARE DESCRIBED AS FOLLOWS:

ANDREW GOODMAN   JAMES EARL CHANEY   MICHAEL HENRY SCHWERNER

An FBI poster sought information on the whereabouts of the missing civil rights campaigners.

travel in groups of mixed races or stand in lighted windows, where they could be easily spotted by gunmen. They learned tactics such as phoning home base at regular times and driving to avoid being followed.

The first wave of volunteers left for Mississippi on June 20. The next day three men were reported missing. They included two white men from the North, Andrew Goodman and Michael Schwerner, and a black Mississippian, James Chaney.

Mississippi had seen dozens of murder cases of black civil rights workers. None of them had prompted a federal investigation. Now with white lives on the line, the federal government began a massive search for the three missing men. "It's tragic," said Rita Schwerner, Michael's wife, "that white northerners have to be caught up into the machinery of injustice and indifference in the South before the American people register concern."

As it turned out, Ku Klux Klan members had murdered the three men to try to scare off the Freedom Summer volunteers. But most volunteers responded with increased resolve. Years later one volunteer called the 1964 summer "the longest nightmare of my life." Volunteers faced the constant threat of violence and arrest.

And they soon realized that their help was not always welcome by frightened African-Americans in rural Mississippi.

In the end the drive registered only 1,600 new black voters. The Freedom Democratic Party also failed to be seated at the Democratic National Convention. Still, Freedom Summer had stirred the conscience of the nation. Even more, a new army of civil rights workers had been tested and come out fighting.

FANNIE LOU HAMER AND THE MFDP

By the end of August 1964, the Mississippi Freedom Democratic Party had about 80,000 members. Among them was Fannie Lou Hamer (below), a disabled woman who had grown up in extreme poverty. Hamer became the face of the new party at the Democratic National Convention.

During her televised testimony, Hamer emotionally recounted how she had been savagely beaten by Mississippi police after a voter registration event. "Is this America, the land of the free and the home of the brave?" she asked.

President Johnson sympathized with Hamer, but he did not want to offend southern white delegates. He needed their votes to win the nomination for another term in office. The president arranged to seat Mississippi's white Democratic "regulars" instead of MFDP delegates.

Hamer was shocked by Johnson's move. But after he was elected, Johnson promised to "eliminate every remaining obstacle" to black voters. The following summer he signed the Voting Rights Act of 1965.

Police beat marchers with clubs in Selma.

THE MARCH TO MONTGOMERY

By early 1965 civil rights workers had joined forces in Selma, Alabama. They came to push for voting rights in a county where fewer than 3 percent of African-Americans were registered to vote. Then in February, Alabama state troopers shot and killed protester Jimmie Lee Jackson as he lunged to protect his mother from a beating.

Selma's black community was at a breaking point. James Bevel of the SCLC had an idea for channeling their anger. He proposed a 54-mile (87-km) march from Selma to Montgomery, the state capital. The march would bring attention to voting rights while expressing outrage at Jackson's death.

About 600 protesters headed east out of Selma on March 7. They sang freedom songs all the way to the top of the Edmund Pettus Bridge. There they took in a heart-stopping sight. On the other side of the bridge was a sea of troopers with gas masks hanging from their belts. Ambulances and hearses stood at the ready. Out of sight were local sheriff James Clark and his men.

Suddenly the troopers attacked. They beat marchers with clubs, shocked them with cattle prods, and blinded them with tear gas. On horseback Clark's men swung at marchers with rubber tubes wrapped with barbed wire. That night ABC broke into regular TV programming to air footage of what came to be known as "Bloody Sunday." The American public watched in horror.

Two days later Martin Luther King Jr. led a second "symbolic" march to the bridge. As expected, state troopers waited again for the marchers on the bridge. This time King led marchers off the bridge before conflict broke out. Many young activists saw his turnaround as a betrayal to the movement.

Finally on March 21, all was clear. President Johnson had sent in federal protection for the protesters. That Sunday morning 3,200 marchers jubilantly stepped across the Edmund Pettus Bridge. Five days later a parade of 25,000 people—white and black—arrived at the Capitol steps in Montgomery. Ten years after the Montgomery bus boycott, the movement had come home.

BENDING TOWARD JUSTICE

The march was the last great victory of King's life. The civil rights movement was changing. Many young activists were drawn to the Black Power Movement, which accepted violence as a strategy.

Stokely Carmichael, head of the Student Nonviolent Coordinating Committee, speaks at a Black Power event in California.

Women also sought more influence in a movement that had mainly been led by men.

The Voting Rights Act was signed into law August 6, 1965. By 1970 most blacks in Alabama and Mississippi could vote. As black officials came into office, the South's old ways began to crumble. But economic and social inequality persisted.

Before King was assassinated in 1968, he had turned his efforts to fighting for the rights of poor people. Before his death, King had shared hopeful words about the hard work ahead. "The arc of the moral universe is long," he said, "but it bends toward justice."

INDEX

INTERNET SITES

Use FactHound to find Internet sites related to this book. All of the sites on FactHound have been researched by our staff.

Here's all you do:
Visit *www.facthound.com*
Type in this code: 9780756547363

GLOSSARY

BAIL—the release of a person from jail until the time of his or her trial

BOYCOTT—an organized refusal to partake in a service or business as a form of protest

CIVIL DISOBEDIENCE—a form of protest in which activists peacefully break the law, often in groups, in order to make a statement

DESEGREGATE—to eliminate any law or practice that separates people on the basis of race

GRASSROOTS—built through massive efforts by ordinary citizens

INTEGRATE—to end the separation of races; desegregate

INTIMIDATION—making someone feel afraid through threats or shows of power

JIM CROW LAWS—state and local laws enforced between the 1880s and the 1960s that separated whites and blacks, especially in southern states

LYNCHING—a public killing by a mob, often by hanging

NONVIOLENCE—the principle of acting peacefully, even in the face of attack

PADDY WAGON—a police van used especially for carrying groups of people to jail

SEGREGATION—the practice, by law or custom, of separating people of different races

TABOO—an action or idea banned by social custom

TIMELINE

1954

May: The U.S. Supreme Court declares school segregation unconstitutional in *Brown v. Board of Education*

1955

August: Emmett Till's shocking murder in Mississippi causes outrage among African-Americans everywhere

December: Bus boycott begins in Montgomery, Alabama, after Rosa Parks refuses to give up her seat to a white passenger

1956

February: Mob prevents Autherine Lucy from crossing color lines at the University of Alabama

1957

September: Nine black teenagers are escorted by federal forces through the doors of Central High School in Little Rock, Arkansas

June: Alabama Governor George Wallace orchestrates a showdown with the Kennedy administration over the admittance of two black students to the University of Alabama

August: Martin Luther King Jr. delivers his "I Have a Dream" speech to a crowd of 250,000 during the March on Washington for Jobs and Freedom

September 1963: Klan members bomb Birmingham's 16th Street Baptist Church, killing four black girls

1964

June: Massive search for three missing Freedom Summer volunteers begins in Mississippi; their bodies are found six weeks later

July: President Lyndon Johnson signs the Civil Rights Act of 1964 into law

August: The Mississippi Freedom Democratic Party fails to be seated at the Democratic

1960

February: Four black college students stage the first sit-in at an all-white lunch counter in Greensboro, North Carolina

1961

May: Mob of angry whites attacks Freedom Riders in Birmingham, Alabama, while police stand by

October: James Meredith becomes the first African-American to enroll at the University of Mississippi

November: Campaign begins to abolish segregation from the small town of Albany, Georgia; it will eventually be considered the biggest failure of Martin Luther King Jr.'s career

1963

May: On Bull Connor's orders, firefighters in Birmingham, Alabama, spray child protesters with fire hoses; images of the day will turn the tide of public opinion in support of the civil rights movement

1965

March: Ten years after the Montgomery bus boycott, marchers from Selma arrive in Montgomery to draw attention to the lack of voting rights for African-Americans

August: The Voting Rights Act of 1965 removes lingering barriers to black voters

Further Reading

Aretha, David. *Martin Luther King Jr. and the 1963 March on Washington.* Greensboro, N.C.: Morgan Reynolds Publishing, 2014.

Levinson, Cynthia. *We've Got a Job: The 1963 Birmingham Children's March.* Atlanta, Ga.: Peachtree Publishers, 2011.

Pinkney, Andrea Davis. *Sit-In: How Four Friends Stood Up by Sitting Down.* New York: Little, Brown and Company, 2010.

Tougas, Shelley. *Little Rock Girl 1957: How a Photograph Changed the Fight for Integration.* Mankato, Minn.: Compass Point Books, 2012.

Select Bibliography

Appiah, Kwame Anthony, and Henry Louis Gates, eds. *Civil Rights: An A to Z Reference to the Movement that Changed America.* Philadelphia, Pa.: Running Press, 2004.

Chappell, David L. *Inside Agitators: White Southerners in the Civil Rights Movement.* Baltimore, Md.: The Johns Hopkins University Press, 1996.

Dierenfield, Bruce J. *The Civil Rights Movement (Seminar Studies in History).* London: Pearson Education Limited, 2008.

Fannie Lou Hamer (1917–1977). 28 Oct. 2013. http://americanradioworks. publicradio.org/features/sayitplain/flhamer.html

Interview with Melba Pattillo Beals. 28 Oct. 2013. http://digital.wustl.edu/cgit/ text/text-idx?c=eop;cc=eop;rgn=main;view=text;idno=bea0015.0713.009

People & Events: Moses and Elizabeth Wright. *American Experience.* 28 Oct. 2013. www.pbs.org/wgbh/amex/till/peopleevents/p_wrights.html

Southern Manifesto on Integration (March 12, 1956). 28 Oct. 2013. www.pbs.org/wnet/supremecourt/rights/sources_document2.html

Wallenfeldt, Jeff, ed. *The Black Experience in America: From Civil Rights to the Present.* New York: Britannica Educational Publishing, 2011.

We Shall Overcome—Historic Places of the Civil Rights Movement. 28 Oct. 2013. www.nps.gov/nr/travel/civilrights/al10.htm

Williams, Juan. *Eyes on the Prize: America's Civil Rights Years 1954–1965.* New York: Penguin Books, 2002.

RACE MIXING IS COMMUNISM

STOP THE RACE MIXING MARCH OF THE CHRIST

RACE MIXING IS COMMUNISM

The Split History of the
CIVIL RIGHTS MOVEMENT

BY NADIA HIGGINS

The News

HIGH COURT BANS SEGREGATION IN PUBLIC

The Split History of the

CIVIL RIGHTS MOVEMENT

SEGREGATIONISTS' PERSPECTIVE

By Nadia Higgins

Content Consultant:
Zoe Burkholder, PhD
Assistant Professor, College of Education and Human Services
Montclair State University

COMPASS POINT BOOKS
a capstone imprint

ABOUT THE AUTHOR:

Nadia Higgins is the author of more than 60 books for children. In addition to the civil rights movement, she has written about other historical topics such as explorers, national parks, inventions, outer space, pop stars, zombies, and more. Higgins lives in Minneapolis, Minnesota, with her husband and two daughters.

SOURCE NOTES:

Activists' Perspective

Page 4, line 5: This Day in History—August 28, 1955: The Death of Emmett Till. 28 Oct. 2013. www.history.com/this-day-in-history/the-death-of-emmett-till

Page 5, line 9: American Experience—People & Events: Moses and Elizabeth Wright. 28 Oct. 2013. www.pbs.org/wgbh/amex/till/peopleevents/p_wrights.html

Page 7, line 12: Juan Williams. *Eyes on the Prize: America's Civil Rights Years 1954–1965*. New York: Penguin Books, 2002, p. 76.

Page 11, line 7: Ibid.

Page 11, line 17: Eyes on the Prize Interviews—Interview with Melba Pattillo Beals. 28 Oct. 2013. http://digital.wustl.edu/cgi/t/text/text-idx?c=eop;cc=eop;rgn=main;view=text;idno=bea0015.0713.009

Page 14, line 3: PBS Newshour—"Jail, No Bail" Stymied Cities Profiting from Civil Rights Protesters. 28 Oct. 2013. www.pbs.org/newshour/bb/social_issues/jan-june11/jail_03-07.html

Page 15, line 9: Bruce J. Dierenfield. *The Civil Rights Movement*. London: Pearson Education Limited, 2008, p. 64.

Page 20, line 10: *Eyes on the Prize: America's Civil Rights Years 1954–1965*, p. 187.

Page 22, line 11: Ibid.

Page 23, line 9: *The Civil Rights Movement*, p. 99.

Page 25, line 18: *Eyes on the Prize: America's Civil Rights Years 1954–1965*, p. 231.

Page 25, line 25: *The Civil Rights Movement*, p. 109.

Page 26, sidebar, line 8: American RadioWorks—Fannie Lou Hamer (1917–1977). 28 Oct. 2013. http://americanradioworks.publicradio.org/features/sayitplain/flhamer.html

Page 26, sidebar, line 19: *Eyes on the Prize: America's Civil Rights Years 1954–1965*, p. 258.

Page 29, line 9: NPR—Theodore Parker and the "Moral Universe." 28 Oct. 2013. www.npr.org/templates/story/story.php?storyId=129609461

Segregationists' Perspective

Page 7, line 23: Bruce J. Dierenfield. *The Civil Rights Movement*. London: Pearson Education Limited, 2008, p. 48.

Page 11, sidebar, line 9: Prairie Public—Southern Manifesto on Integration (March 12, 1956). 28 Oct. 2013. www.pbs.org/wnet/supremecourt/rights/sources_document2.html

Page 11, line 6: Juan Williams. *Eyes on the Prize: America's Civil Rights Years 1954–1965*. New York: Penguin Books, 2002, p. 97.

Page 13, line 2: Ibid.

Page 16, line 5: Ibid.

Page 18, line 7: Gene Howard. *Patterson for Alabama: The Life and Career of John Patterson*. Tuscaloosa: University of Alabama Press, 2008, p. 195.

Page 20, line 1: *Eyes on the Prize: America's Civil Rights Years 1954–1965*, p. 174.

Page 20, line 9: David L. Chappell. *Inside Agitators: White Southerners in the Civil Rights Movement*. Baltimore, Md.: The Johns Hopkins University Press, 1996, p. 131.

Page 21, line 10: *The Civil Rights Movement*, p. 72.

Page 22, line 14: *Eyes on the Prize: America's Civil Rights Years 1954–1965*, p. 217.

Page 23, line 3: NPR—"Segregation Forever": A Fiery Pledge Forgiven, But Not Forgotten. 28 Oct. 2013. www.npr.org/2013/01/14/169080969/segregation-forever-a-fiery-pledge-forgiven-but-not-forgotten

Page 27, line 7: Wayne Greenhaw. *Fighting the Devil in Dixie: How Civil Rights Activists Took on the Ku Klux Klan in Alabama*. Chicago: Chicago Review Press, 2011, p. 255.

Page 29, line 6: *Eyes on the Prize: America's Civil Rights Years 1954–1965*, p. 273.

Table of Contents

CH. 1 TROUBLE STIRRING

*B*lack Monday." To southern segregationists that was how May 17, 1954, would be remembered. On that day the U.S. Supreme Court ruled in *Brown v. Board of Education* that African-American children had a constitutional right to attend school with white children.

Most southern whites reacted with shock, defiance, and fear. Their congressmen banged their fists and shouted with rage from the halls of government. Southern governors promised to shut down schools rather than see them integrated.

Female Klan members gather in front of a burning cross.

After *Brown*, men in white hoods packed Ku Klux Klan rallies. The hate group took violent revenge on black citizens they perceived as "uppity." Any black man who tried to register to vote or who looked a white woman in the eye was a target for lynching.

The *Brown* decision also spurred a new kind of hate group. While poor, rural men flocked to Klan rituals, businessmen filled the rolls at White Citizens' Council meetings. These "white-collar Klansmen" attacked with economic weapons. They might, for example, arrange for a black man who tried to enroll his child at a white school to be fired. Or he might have his rent raised.

"OUR WAY OF LIFE"

With violence and economic punishments, many southern whites intimidated blacks into keeping their "proper" place. But they also had two other powerful weapons—law and custom. Jim Crow laws segregated public spaces. Southern whites and blacks drank from different water fountains, traveled separately, and dined in different restaurants. Custom dictated that a black man never looked a white woman in the eye. Both law and custom kept blacks away from voting booths and the institutions of power.

To many white southerners, the *Brown* decision was an attack on a way of life they had enjoyed for 300 years. Generations of white

Water coolers were segregated throughout the South.

southerners had grown up believing that African-Americans were inferior. Their interpretation of the Bible and their ideas about race justified these deeply held views.

And now, all of a sudden, change was being imposed from outside—from northerners who had ignored racial inequality in the South for decades. Many southerners heard echoes of the Civil War defeat ringing in the Supreme Court's decree. But another practical matter was as stake. If black and white children sat side by side at school, they might grow up thinking of themselves as equals. That could lead to blacks and whites marrying and having children together, and this was the most feared of all southern taboos.

AGITATORS IN MONTGOMERY

Many whites in Montgomery, Alabama, were shaking their heads in disbelief in December 1955. Rosa Parks, a 42-year-old black woman, had broken the law by refusing to give up her seat to a white passenger on a crowded bus.

Four days later, on December 5, the buses in Montgomery were practically empty. The black community was boycotting the buses, and a young preacher named Martin Luther King Jr. was leading their raucous meetings. Most whites believed that King, a newcomer, had no business causing trouble in their town.

A boycott was bad news for the bus company, which relied mostly on fares from black riders. But Mayor W.A. "Tacky" Gayle wasn't worried. "Comes the first rainy day and the Negroes will be back on the buses," he said.

A bus is nearly empty during the 1956 Montgomery bus boycott.

But as days, weeks, and then months passed, Gayle and others had to admit that the boycott was not going away. In fact the activists had increased their demands. Now they were calling for complete desegregation of city buses. A fight was on, and city officials could not risk a black victory. If blacks won this time, what would they ask for next?

By November 1956, after 11 months, Montgomery had lost about $1 million to the boycott. That month the U.S. Supreme Court ordered Montgomery to desegregate its buses. Montgomery's white rulers had not given in, but they had been defeated.

"WE ARE OCCUPIED TERRITORY"

CH. 2

Autherine Lucy prompted an angry white mob when she tried to break the color barrier at the University of Alabama in February 1956. Soon after Lucy was expelled for accusing university officials of not keeping order. Lucy's case showed that mob violence did indeed block integration. Segregationists also took note that President Dwight Eisenhower had not used federal might to enforce the *Brown* ruling and ensure Lucy's attendance. The following year, however, *Brown* would be tested again with a far different outcome.

-9-

Autherine Lucy (left, front), with her lawyers, won a court battle to enroll in the University of Alabama but was expelled days later.

ORVAL FAUBUS' POLITICAL GAMBLE

Arkansas governor Orval Faubus worried that his soft stance on race was becoming a political hazard. Faubus had presided over the integration of colleges in his home state. But now, in 1957, with elections coming up, polls were showing that Faubus would have to harden his stance to stay in office.

That summer Faubus saw his chance with a case at Little Rock's Central High School. Little Rock city officials were already doing what they could to discourage integration. New laws required black students to fill out extra paperwork to attend an all-white school. Local parents even organized a phone drive. Volunteers telephoned

"SOUTHERN MANIFESTO"

One hundred and one southern members of the U.S. Congress took a defiant stand against the *Brown* decision on segregated schools in March 1956. Representing every state of the former Confederacy, the congressmen signed a document now known as the Southern Manifesto. The document called the *Brown* ruling a "clear abuse of judicial power" that trampled states' cherished rights. It warned of the chaos and confusion that would result from such unlawful policy. In later decades having signed the Southern Manifesto became a mark of shame on a southern politician's career.

Senator Strom Thurmond (right) prepares a draft of the Southern Manifesto.

black parents to talk them out of risking their children's safety by sending them to all-white schools.

The actions were backed up by the threat of violence. Angry whites sent a rock flying through the living room window of Daisy Bates, the activist who was spearheading integration efforts. A note tied to the rock warned, "Stone this time, dynamite next." By the end of August, the list of about 75 black teenagers who had signed up for Central High had been pared down to just nine.

Daisy Bates gazes through a window in her home that was broken by segregationists.

Governor Faubus introduced another tactic September 2. He appeared on TV, warning of coming mayhem should integration go forward. He announced that he was sending National Guardsmen to Little Rock to maintain order. On September 4, however, the soldiers' true mission was revealed. That day the soldiers physically prevented the nine black teenagers from passing through school doors. For the first time since the Civil War, a state had blocked the will of the federal government.

An angry mob prevented the Little Rock Nine from attending Central High again on September 23. Despite President Eisenhower's urgings, Faubus would not protect the students. Finally, on September 24, Eisenhower reluctantly sent in federal troops to escort the black students into the school.

People around the nation watched as soldiers in helicopters and armed jeeps did what Faubus had refused to do. "We are now an occupied territory," Faubus defiantly cried.

The next year Faubus closed high schools in Little Rock entirely rather than see black and white students mix. He also won his third term as governor by a landslide. A Gallup Poll in late 1958 named Faubus one of the 10 most admired men in America. Across the South politicians took note. Orval Faubus' political gamble had paid off.

Arkansas Governor Orval Faubus shows his support for segregation in 1958.

RETALIATION AND INTIMIDATION

usiness owners in Nashville, Tennessee, were starting to

get desperate in the spring of 1960. The "sit-in" movement that had

spread across the South was especially strong in their city. The

trouble had begun the previous winter. About 200 black students

had refused to budge from whites-only lunch counters in downtown

department stores on February 18.

At first segregationists claimed that sit-ins were just the latest

college fad. The black students were looking for publicity—and were

getting plenty of it. Business owners responded mostly by ignoring the

protests. Some managers roped off their lunch counters entirely, while

others pressured local colleges to expel the activists.

Sit-in protesters are attacked at a lunch counter in Jackson, Mississippi.

But as the sit-ins continued, angry whites began attacking the
black students. Crowded paddy wagons rolled down Nashville's
streets as police arrested the students on charges such as trespassing
or disturbing the peace. Soon white customers were afraid to shop
downtown, while black customers refused to spend their money at
the segregated stores.

In desperation, business owners proposed opening black
sections at the lunch counters, but the activists refused the offer.
They wanted nothing less than full integration. Then, on April 19,
angry whites bombed the home of one of the city's prominent
black lawyers. That same day Nashville's citizens looked on in

astonishment as a crowd of 2,500 activists silently marched to Nashville's City Hall.

Mayor Ben West was waiting for them on the building's steps. One protester asked him about his personal beliefs on the sit-ins. West looked into the thousands of expectant faces. "I found that I had to answer it frankly and honestly," he later recalled. "I did not agree that it was morally right for someone to sell them merchandise and refuse them service."

Privately Nashville business owners breathed a sigh of relief. Less than a month later, lunch counters were opened up to black customers. The struggling stores could get back to business, while Mayor West shouldered the blame.

MOB RULE

Just as the sit-ins were winding down, new trouble cropped up in the South. Civil rights workers were staging Freedom Rides to defy segregation's rules on interstate buses and bus terminals. The Freedom Rides introduced a new twist: Here came white activists to sing songs in the back of the bus and walk brazenly into "colored" facilities. That was more than some whites could abide.

A mob of Klansmen was waiting for a Freedom Ride bus in Birmingham, Alabama, the afternoon of May 14, 1961. Eugene "Bull" Connor, the city's public safety commissioner, had promised the Klan a full 15 minutes to attack the riders before officers would break up the fray. As riders stepped off the bus, Klan members clubbed and whipped them with bats, pipes, and bicycle chains.

Freedom Riders hang signs out the windows as they head to Washington, D.C.

Connor and the Klansmen had expected the attack to end the bus tour, but new riders were coming to Birmingham to continue it. The matter was now in the hands of Governor John Patterson. The Freedom Rides were gathering international media attention. President John F. Kennedy's administration was pressuring the governor to protect the riders and defuse the embarrassing situation as quietly as possible. That enraged Patterson. In his view the president should be working to stop the real troublemakers—the Freedom Riders themselves.

For several days Patterson simply refused to return the president's phone calls. Finally the governor issued a vague statement about protecting all people on Alabama's highways.

National Guardsmen, who replaced U.S. marshals, remained alert as Freedom Riders boarded a bus in Montgomery May 24, 1961.

State troopers escorted the Freedom Riders out of Birmingham on May 20. However, as the buses closed in on Montgomery, the patrol cars suddenly disappeared. Awaiting Klansmen in Montgomery freely carried out another attack on the riders.

The Kennedy administration felt tricked by Patterson. It immediately sent in U.S. marshals to restore order in Montgomery. Ever defiant, Patterson told reporters, "Now the federal government comes in here and illegally interferes in a domestic situation they themselves helped to create."

The Freedom Riders left Alabama accompanied by planes, helicopters, and police cars on May 24. The Freedom Rides continued without another attack that summer. In the fall a federal ruling outlawed segregation on interstate buses and terminals. Mob rule had failed as a segregationist strategy.

SOUTHERN DIE-HARDS

When civil rights activists arrived in Albany, Georgia, in late 1961, police chief Laurie Pritchett was ready. Pritchett had read up on the movement's nonviolent strategies. He knew, for example, that the protesters were counting on filling up Albany's jails as a way to stop arrests. So Pritchett called officers at neighboring towns and asked to use their jails.

Pritchett told his men that in no way were they to appear rough with protesters. That would only attract negative media attention. The officers were tested July 24, 1962, when angry protesters pelted

Police Chief Laurie Pritchett often worked 20-hour days during the protests.

them with rocks and bottles. The police did not fight back. "Did you see them nonviolent rocks?" Pritchett smugly asked reporters. The classic image of nonviolent protester versus white southern thug was turned on its head.

Earlier that month the wily Pritchett had arranged to pay Martin Luther King Jr.'s bail when King's jail sentence was starting to receive attention from President Kennedy. In August 1962 King left Albany with segregation intact. Pritchett could not take all the credit, but he was certainly a factor. As he put it, "We met 'nonviolence' with 'nonviolence,' and we are indeed proud of the outcome."

ROSS BARNETT

Mississippi governor Ross Barnett was at a low point in his career in 1961. A scandal had broken out over gold-plated faucet handles in his mansion and other luxuries he enjoyed. A crowd had even heckled him during a University of Mississippi football game. But one year later, Barnett stood triumphantly on the 50-yard line as the crowd wildly cheered him.

Like many before him, Barnett had found a cure for his political ills in segregation. In early September 1962, a federal court ordered that African-American James Meredith be enrolled at the University of Mississippi. "Never!" Barnett shouted.

Barnett personally blocked the door as Meredith tried to enroll at the university on September 25. The governor was then faced

Mississippi Lieutenant Governor Paul Johnson (left) tells a U.S. marshal that James Meredith (right) won't be admitted to the University of Mississippi.

U.S. marshals travel through the Mississippi campus to enforce a federal court order that James Meredith be admitted to the university.

with the threat of arrest unless he allowed Meredith to proceed. As white supporters stood guard at Barnett's mansion, Barnett looked for a way to save face.

He telephoned U.S. Attorney General Bobby Kennedy and proposed a deal. Barnett suggested that the federal marshals escorting Meredith draw their guns and pretend to force the state police to give in. Not only did Kennedy refuse, he threatened to leak a transcript of their phone call to the public. A terrified Barnett privately agreed to let Meredith register but vowed to remain defiant in public.

Meredith did register on October 1, but only after a riot erupted on the campus. For 14 hours a frenzied mob of 3,000 charged at federal marshals. At the height of riot, Barnett went on the radio. He shouted, "I call on Mississippi to keep the faith and courage. We will never surrender."

GEORGE WALLACE

Alabama's new governor George Wallace (below) whipped the crowd into a fervor at his inauguration speech in January 1963. "Segregation now, segregation tomorrow, and segregation forever," he declared. The formerly moderate politician vowed to stand in every Alabama schoolhouse door to uphold segregation.

Wallace did stand in one "schoolhouse door" at the University of Alabama on June 11, 1963. His stated goal was to prevent two black students from enrolling. In truth Wallace was looking for a showdown. As TV cameras rolled, Wallace raised his hand, halting the students' white escort in his tracks. Wallace then read a statement blasting the federal government's intrusion. Once President Kennedy took command of Alabama's National Guard, Wallace backed down.

With that show of defiance, Wallace's political career took off. He won an unprecedented three more terms as Alabama governor and ran for president four times. Wallace became confined to a wheelchair in 1972 after an assassination attempt paralyzed him from the waist down. Ten years later he publically apologized for his former racist views. He died in 1998.

DESPERATE MEASURES
CH. 5

Almost half of Mississippi's citizens were African-American in the 1960s. Klan groups and White Citizens' Councils were also more powerful there. Backed by local government, they kept blacks "in their place"—and out of voting booths. So when Mississippi became the target for a major voter registration drive in 1964, the state's white racists were livid. They especially resented young white northerners coming in to challenge cherished southern traditions.

When the first Freedom Summer volunteers arrived in late June, Klan members outside the small town of Philadelphia were waiting

Klan members burn a cross at one of their meetings.

for them. The hate group had recently burned down a local church for agreeing to host a "freedom school." The fire served as both a warning and a lure. Klan leaders knew that volunteers would come to investigate the site.

Sure enough, three volunteers drove out to the church on June 21. On their way back, the county's deputy sheriff, Cecil Ray Price, arrested them on fake traffic charges. Price took the three to jail, only to release them into the hands of his fellow Klansmen. Klan members gunned the three workers down, and then buried their bodies under 30 feet (9 meters) of mud.

Six weeks later federal agents found the bodies. Nineteen white men were arrested, but the state refused to charge them with murder. Eventually Price and six others were convicted of a lesser charge by the U.S. Justice Department. Still, for the first time ever, a Mississippi jury convicted a Klan member in connection with the death of a black man.

BLOODY SUNDAY

Mayor Joseph Smitherman of Selma, Alabama, was getting worried. He had heard that Martin Luther King Jr. was arriving in town to lead a voter registration movement. Smitherman feared his hot-headed sheriff, James Clark, would create a crisis similar to the one in Birmingham in 1963.

Protesters sought shelter in a doorway while being hosed by a fireman in Birmingham May 3, 1963.

THE 16TH STREET CHURCH BOMBING

In September 1963 Klan members in Birmingham, Alabama, were plotting what would become known as the worst crime of the era. Earlier that month five of the city's black children had enrolled at white schools. On Saturday, September 14, Klansmen Robert Chambliss boasted to his niece, "You just wait until after Sunday morning. And they will beg us to let them segregate." The next morning a bomb ripped through the 16th Street Baptist Church, killing four black girls.

Within weeks Chambliss and three others were identified as suspects, but the FBI did not have enough evidence to bring them to trial. Fourteen years after the bombing, in 1977, Chambliss was convicted of murder, thanks in part to his niece's testimony. Two other bombers, Thomas E. Blanton Jr. and Bobby Frank Cherry, were convicted in 2001 and 2002.

Smitherman called King and tried to convince him not to come. When that failed Smitherman leaned on Clark to show restraint, as unlikely as that seemed. Then, in February 1965, Clark punched a civil rights worker so hard, the sheriff broke one of his fingers.

Smitherman's fear of a crisis became a reality at the Edmund Pettus Bridge on March 7, 1965. Activists had just begun a 54-mile (87-kilometer) march from Selma to Montgomery. George Wallace, Alabama's governor, had banned the march, claiming it would disrupt highway traffic.

State troopers slapped billy clubs against their hands as they faced the activists on the bridge. Major John Cloud gave the

State troopers swing clubs to break up a civil rights voting march in Selma on March 7.

marchers two minutes to retreat, but they refused to budge.

What happened next would come to be known as Bloody Sunday. Troopers beat marchers with clubs and cattle prods. Sheriff Clark's men chased protesters on horseback and pushed them off the bridge. That night ABC TV aired footage from Bloody Sunday. As Smitherman put it, "The wrath of the nation came down on us."

Governor Wallace still refused to offer police protection for the marchers. He claimed the state could not afford the expense. President Lyndon Johnson took control of Alabama's National Guard on March 21, and the five-day march went forward under heavy protection. Major Cloud and Sheriff Clark led the march in a patrol car for part of the way. Clark saved face by telling reporters he was relieved to get the troublemakers out of town.

A NEW SOUTH

The Voting Rights Act of 1965 removed barriers to black voters. Soon about 60 percent of Selma's African-Americans had registered to vote, and Sheriff Clark was ousted. That pattern would continue across the South—black officials and white moderates took the place of old-school segregationists.

As their constituencies changed, some segregationists changed their tunes. They began courting the black vote. Some seemed genuinely sorry for their actions. George Wallace personally apologized to Rosa Parks, John Lewis, and other heroes of the civil rights movement. Segregation had been a political trump card in the old South. Now it had become a new taboo.

INDEX